A lifelong fan of road ra[...]
of the first people to wri[...]
and its fans seriously. His [...]
passionate and incisive commentary – published in
eight bestselling books – provide an unrivalled
chronicle of road racing.

His early books, *Beautiful Danger*, *Ragged Edge* and
Hard Roads, now available for the first time in
paperback, are highly sought-after classics.

Much has changed since the books were first
published – the greater professionalism of the sport,
the increased focus on safety, and the renaissance of
the TT. Races have come and gone, and so too have
some of the much-loved riders whose talent and skill
are captured in the pages of these books.

Davison, meanwhile, has remained involved, both
professionally and personally, in the ebb and flow of
the sport's fortunes. He has worked alongside those
who have sought to influence change while continuing
to document every aspect of road racing as a
journalist and photographer.

The enduring appeal of *Beautiful Danger*, *Ragged
Edge* and *Hard Roads* lies not just in the stories and
incredible photographs that the books contain, but in
the fact they make us reflect on the road travelled
and on why the sport matters so much.

Martin Finnegan leaps his JMF Millsport Yamaha over Black's Farm Jump at the 2008 Cookstown 100.

Hard Roads

STEPHEN DAVISON

THE ROAD RACING SEASON AT FULL THROTTLE

BLACKSTAFF
PRESS
—
BELFAST

Peering from behind a red flag, Joey Dunlop waits for the start of practice at the North West 200.

On the evening after Martin Finnegan lost his life in a crash at the Tandragee 100 in 2008, I left the course to drive north towards home. Initially the roads were unfamiliar, and the twists and turns held no landmarks that I knew, nothing to temper the alienation and sadness of that tragic day.

As I neared home the countryside became more familiar. The corners now had names that I knew, the houses and fields were places I had worked in or visited. These were my roads, the passageways of my life, where down the years I had travelled to school, to my wedding, to my daughters' births, to my father's funeral. They were the places where I grew up and lived much of my life; the byways where I learned to ride a bicycle and a motorbike, passed my driving test and found the freedom that the road offers. Behind these hedges we had saved hay and gathered potatoes, lifted stones and made fences. Woven into the very fabric of my life, I may never get lost on these byways but I often get lost in the remembering.

On the night of my friend's death these roads offered comfort, and I was glad of it.

Martin Finnegan lived his twenty-nine years surrounded by similar roads and he was drawn to race on them. He won numerous races on the lanes that comprise the Skerries and Killalane courses close to where he grew up in Lusk, County Dublin. But for Martin, in his chosen profession, the ordinary and familiar represented great danger. The very things that offer security and comfort along the routes of our daily lives – the footpaths that lead our children to school, the telephone poles that carry the conversations between neighbours, hedges that hold in our gardens, fences that enclose the fields, the streetlights that guide us on our way – can become a final resting place in a blinding moment for a road racer.

Sitting at a race with my camera waiting for the bikes to appear, I often ponder the irony of how the surroundings can so quickly become the scene of carnage if things go wrong. Shaded by trees in the stillness, with cattle standing in the fields, birds singing and the sweet smell of grass all around, I am enveloped in an ordinary beauty. Fearful anticipation grows with the roar of the approaching bikes and the excitement of the incredible spectacle is always tempered with relief at the riders' safe passing. That bittersweet sensation is ever-present in road racing – excitement and fear, triumph and disaster, beauty and danger. All of life – and death – is encompassed here and it provides the sport with its deepest fascination.

That fascination begins with the road, for racer and photographer alike. In the bright times when I am recording happy moments of camaraderie and victory, those roads are easy places to be, full of the fun and life of the sport. On other, darker days they are much more difficult places to be – tougher, unforgiving and callous.

Hard roads.

Guy Martin (Hydrex Honda) emerges from the shadows
at Braddan Bridge during the 2007 Isle of Man TT.

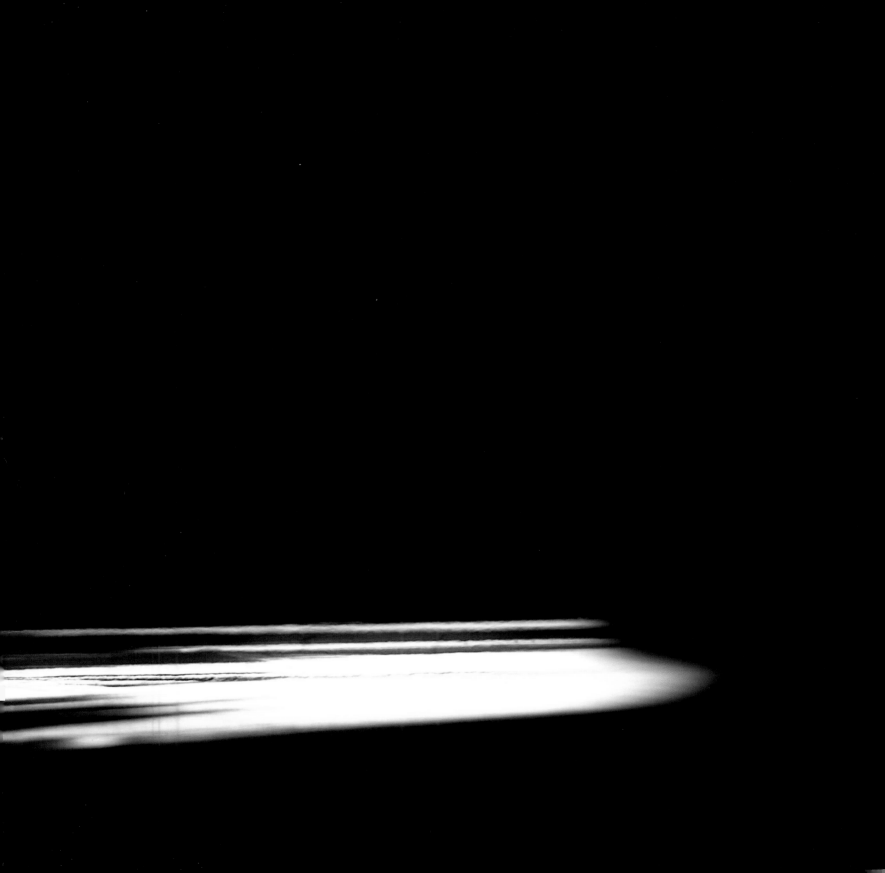

Cookstown
100

It won't come as any surprise to road race fans to discover that the original Cookstown 100, scheduled for 4 May 1922, was abandoned because of heavy rain. The traditional Irish season curtain-raiser in County Tyrone is often dogged by poor weather as heavy spring showers douse the spectators and make tyre choice a lottery for the racers.

Much has changed in the eighty-odd years since the race began, including numerous course changes and a huge reduction in the race distance. The old titles of '100' and '150' that many of the Irish races still maintain in their names refer to the miles covered in the days when races were run as handicap events with staggered starting times, depending on machine and rider ability. Today, the Cookstown is run over a 2.1-mile course on the outskirts of the town with racers completing eight or so laps of the circuit.

Of course, nowadays races are much, much faster, with a dozen or more 200bhp machines battling between hedges often not much wider apart than an average family saloon car, and all from a mass start outside the Braeside Inn. The pub is an essential component of almost every Irish road race and while Breathalyser tests ensure that the riders stay alcohol-free until the post-race party, the fans can wet their whistles as they watch the charge to the chequered flag just yards from the pub door.

John Burrows shaves the privet hedges at Mackney Corner on his HM Motorhomes Suzuki during the 600cc race at the 2008 Cookstown.

For most road racers the winter months are a series of long nights spent in sheds and garages preparing the bikes for the season ahead. In a sport where only a handful make their living from racing, balancing the pressures of a full working day with the demands of family life and preparation for racing is a line finely trod.

Intent on making precise adjustments to the front brakes of his R1 Yamaha, Waterford road racer Dave Coughlan might not even notice his daughter Clara's little hand on his leg, but it is there, offering reassurance and tenderness in a sport that is so often uncertain and brutal in its effects. The four-year-old might not see as much of her daddy as she would like, as his time is eaten up with his day job and the racing he loves, but when he is at home in the garage with his spanners she is there, by his side and close.

Under pressure, Martin Finnegan sweats out the final seconds of a blood-oxygen test in the Sports Science department of Limerick University in February 2008. In the old days riders had a much more llaid-back attitude to issues such as fitness and nutrition but there has been a shift in this approach in recent years and nowadays the top riders season ahead. That season includes gruelling physical tests such as six-lap races of the 37 3/4-mile Isle of Man TT course and fitness is now a top priority in a sport where chip butties and beer were once the staple diet.

The modern world, if a little slowly, has finally caught up with pure road racing.

Almost all of the bends, jumps and features of any closed public road course are named after commonly held local associations; the name of the townland or local resident or, as in this case, the name of the local farmer. Black's Farm is a colloquial reference point for 364 days of the year but on the day of the Cookstown 100 it becomes the name of one of the most spectacular vantage points in Irish road racing, as this picture of Richard Britton in 2005 on the DMRR Honda illustrates.

Some spectators take photographs, some wave encouragement and some simply watch as Darren Burns skims round the approach to Black's Farm on his 250cc Honda right under their noses at Cookstown in 2008.

Ireland has a huge following of race fans, many of whom are immensely knowledgeable about the sport and its history. They are drawn back year after year to places like this where the proximity to the speed and action is unknown in any other sport.

For all have sinned, and come short of the glory of God

Romans 3:23

Tandragee
100

1958 saw the first Tandragee 100 run on the present course in north Armagh, and many regard it as the last 'true' National Irish road race course. The conflicting demands of keeping increasingly intolerant residents happy and marshalling long circuits has led to a drive towards shorter courses. At over 5 miles long, Tandragee stands alone as a throwback to an older time. Fast and flowing for most of its miles with a tight 'back road' section and a big jump, Tandragee has it all.

Cameron Donald is from Australia and he knew nothing of this history, having never seen Tandragee before 3 May 2006, and he had never read any of the 'good living' messages on our Ulster telegraph poles either. He probably didn't see much of this sign on race day as he was concentrating so hard on winning races and setting lap records at the start of a season that no one remembers ever having seen the like of before.

Every weekend throughout the early summer Cameron arrived at courses that were steeped in road racing tradition, places where the greats had cut their teeth before they made their mark. Cameron's mark was both instant and stunning. At Tandragee, Kells, Skerries and Walderstown he won and set outright lap records within hours of arrival.

Cameron Donald exits Bell's Crossroads on the Duncan Honda during the 2006 Tandragee 100.

Road racers love to see pictures of themselves in action, to see how far they lean over, how high they have taken the jump. For me the moments of purest pleasure in my photography come in sharing the pictures with the men who made them; reminiscing, laughing, pondering. That is how I would want it to be, to be able to grow old with the racers and share in the remembering, but in this perilous sport that chance is so often denied.

Since this picture of the Open race grid at the 2007 Tandragee was taken two men are gone. John Donnan (12) was killed later that day, only yards from the spot where he is sitting. A year later Martin Finnegan (45) died in another crash at Tandragee.

No one feels the loss like the families of these men. But we are all cheated by their passing, cheated of the chance to share with them the times of our lives that they have brightened immeasurably. In those bleak moments of loss the roads never seem so hard.

One of the nicest things about going to a road race is the way that, in some respects, time seems to stand still. Ever since I was a youngster there have been men wearing tweed overcoats like Sammy Gault, complete with shirt and tie and working-man's boots, standing in hedges the length and breadth of this country.

A few minutes after I had taken this photograph of Martin Finnegan in action during practice for the 2008 Tandragee 100, he rang me. He had finished the practice session and stepped off his bike back at the paddock. Even though he had been racing over Cooley Hill Jump at 100mph Martin had spotted me in the hedge and he wanted to know if I had got the picture of him – sure hadn't he looked over at my camera and everything! I told him that I had and that he had scared the living daylights out of me too. We laughed and said that we would meet up the following day.

As I walked towards Martin on the grid the next morning I asked him if he had seen that morning's paper with his picture in it. 'Magic!' he said with a huge grin. Martin was in great form that morning, laughing with the mechanics and chatting with the rest of the folk waiting for the race to begin. As he pulled on his helmet I raised my camera to capture it but he was too quick for me. Martin saw I had missed the shot and he pulled the helmet off again and gave me this smile. It was to be the last photograph I would take of him, the last words we would share, as he was killed instantly in a crash just a few miles down the road at Marlacoo Corner.

Over the previous few years I had followed Martin Finnegan around the world, taking his picture as we lived the road racing life to the full. He was, simply, the most spectacular road racer there has ever been and capturing those moments created some of the best pictures I have ever taken. There are a million cherished memories but for now it is impossible to accept that there will be no more 'Did you get it?' phone calls from Martin.

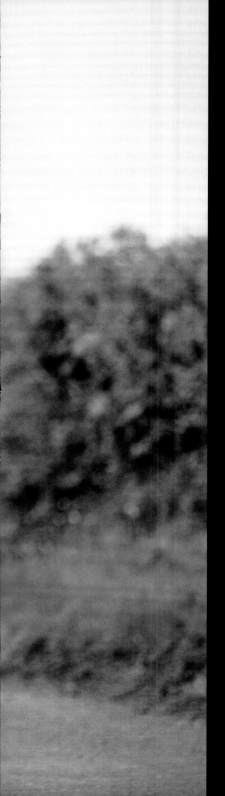

North West 200

Regarded as safer than the Isle of Man TT, the North West 200, the first of the four International race meetings, has become the most popular road racing event in the world with some one hundred thousand people visiting Northern Ireland's north coast to watch the May races. The nine-mile triangle encompassing Portrush, Portstewart and Coleraine is superfast. Michael Rutter hit over 200mph here in 2005, the fastest speed ever recorded in a motorcycle race in these islands. Chicanes have had to be utilised to slow the bikes and nowadays the racing at the North West has become more akin to track racing, with every race being closely contested by a group of riders who set off in a mass start.

It is incredible to think that Ireland's biggest sporting event is still essentially run by a small group of unpaid volunteers in the Coleraine and District Motor Club. As with all road races, there is a huge dependency on people who work for the love of the sport and the current race supremo Mervyn Whyte relies on an army of volunteers to carry out every task, from setting up the course to selling programmes. Over four thousand safety bales and several miles of protective fencing have to be erected and removed from the course each year. These volunteers work around the clock in the weeks leading up to the race, juggling their day jobs with their efforts to ensure the North West 200 runs smoothly. The aim for everyone involved is a safe and successful day's racing.

Racing in the streets. Stephen Thompson (6, T&R Suzuki) and Bruce Anstey (5, TAS Suzuki) lead the Superstock pack into York Hairpin at Portstewart on the coast road in 2006.

Ian Lougher stands the Stobart Honda on its end as he comes over
Black Hill at the North West 200 in 2006.

Top road racers are often quoted as saying that they ride at nine-tenths of their control,
keeping something back, racing within some kind of personal limit that gives a nod to the
dangers of the road. No such thoughts seem to have been reining in Les Shand on the AIM
Yamaha at the North West 200 in 2005. On a day of sunshine and showers there was the
odd puddle left where the heat had not dried the road completely. A patch of water on the
approach to this bend coated Shand's rear tyre. As soon as the power went on, the back end
came round and the young Scot just rode the drift towards the kerb.

The speed-limit signs are ignored as Ian Lougher (2, Black Horse Honda) leads the Supersport pack off the line and down into the first corner at Mill Bank during the 2006 North West 200.

Australian Cameron Donald (Uel Duncan Honda) leads Davy Morgan (DMRR Honda) out of York Hairpin in the Superstock race during the 2006 North West 200. Donald had crashed twice during practice and was racing with a broken ankle.

Richard Britton (P.J. O'Kane Suzuki) leads David Jefferies (TAS Suzuki) through the railway bridge at Dhu Varren during a wet Supersport race at the 2002 North West 200. The marshals ensure that no spectators venture on to the railway embankment or railway track but this was not always so and in times gone by this whole area was crowded with race fans.

The coast road between Portrush and Portstewart is at the heart of the North West course and attracts the greatest number of spectators to the caravan parks and bars that line the way to the paddock.

Ryan Farquhar kicks up the stones as he rides his Harker Kawasaki right into the gutter beside the kerb at the start and finish chicane in the Superstock race at the 2005 North West 200.

Richard Britton and Ian Lougher douse Superbike race winner Bruce Anstey in champagne on the podium at the 2005 North West 200.

In 2008 the promotion of the North West 200 took a new direction with the launch of a race team called North West 200 Ducati. The team, with Michael Rutter on board, competed in the British Superbike championship before winning its debut race on the Triangle course.

Robert Dunlop enjoys a joke while working in his garage in 1998.

Robert Dunlop smiles from inside his helmet straight into my camera as he prepares to leave the grid in the 250cc session on the Thursday evening practice for the 2008 North West 200. Robert had not ridden a 250cc machine at the North West since his crash at the Isle of Man TT in 1994 left him struggling to manage anything bigger than a 125cc bike. He had won the 125cc race at the 2006 meeting to secure his position as the most successful North West rider of all time with fifteen wins. In 2008 he wanted to add to his tally by riding in both the 250cc and 125cc races.

After the bikes left the line on Thursday evening I ran up through the grid to the final corner to photograph Robert as he completed the lap but he never came back. His machine seized at Mather's Cross and the Ballymoney man lost his life in the crash.

The elder statesman of road racing, Robert Dunlop lived to race and his sheer strength of mind and will had seen him hit every height the sport has to offer in spite of injury. With his brother Joey, Robert had dominated Irish road racing for the previous thirty years and he fostered the continuance of the Dunlop dynasty in the sport through his sons William and Michael. As a huge cloud descended upon the 2008 North West 200 with Robert's death it was the bravery of the Dunlop youngsters that raised everyone's spirits.

Michael Dunlop wheelies the Pirate Racing 250cc Honda out of the start and finish chicane on his way to victory in the 250cc race at the 2008 North West 200.

With their father dead and not yet buried, both William and Michael Dunlop chose to ride in the 250cc race in his honour on the Saturday morning of the North West race day. Concerned officials were understandably uncomfortable about their decision but the pair were determined to race. Unfortunately, William's bike broke down on the warm-up lap, leaving Michael to compete alone. The Ballymoney youngster displayed all of the famous Dunlop grit as he battled throughout the race with Christian Elkin and John McGuinness before taking the chequered flag to win the most emotional motorcycle race Ireland has ever witnessed. Overcome by emotion, Michael collapsed and had to be carried to the podium.

Robert Dunlop epitomised the 'get on with it' attitude that is so much a part of the road racing scene. He had suffered the death of his brother and brother-in-law as well as numerous friends. Racing had inflicted serious

and crippling injuries upon him but through it all Robert had battled on, doing what he loved. In the very darkest days, the sport looked to Robert for guidance and inspiration. If he could go on, so could we.

The North West paddock was dark and cold on that fateful Thursday night when Robert Dunlop lost his life, and it seemed that the licence to keep going that he had provided had been revoked. But Robert had already created his legacy. He had instilled in his two racing sons, William and Michael, and in his other son Daniel, who was serving with the British Army in Iraq and Afghanistan, the same force of will and determination that he had so often displayed himself.

Michael's victory was not just a race win – it was a triumph over a tragedy that was personal to all of us in the road racing family, and if he could do that then couldn't we go on too?

Isle of Man TT

In 2007 the Isle of Man TT celebrated its centenary, making it not just the most prestigious road race in the world but also the oldest. Although the TT has been experiencing major change and development in the last few years, the thing that is the very essence of the event remains unchanged; the incredible 37³/₄-mile long Mountain course. While the quality of facilities is important, the crowd and the atmosphere give the event life, and the riders are the people who make it all happen, it is the course itself that is at the heart of the TT races. When you first drive or ride the course you are struck by its sheer length; you seem to have been going for ages and you haven't even made halfway. In those 37 miles the scenery and surroundings change dramatically from forest glen to village street to mountain road. If you listen to someone like John McGuinness talk about the course in detail it becomes apparent that it is a living, organic thing that changes from day to day, mile to mile. There is no substitute for experience on the Mountain course. A rider like John doesn't bother doing low-speed laps in a car or road bike – 'There's no point going round at 40mph and having time to see all the things that you could hit at 140mph,' he says. The top riders are aware of every bump and manhole cover, of the places where the back wheel will spin up, or the spots to be avoided in the damp. All of this has to be learnt, remembered, and then put to use to lap at an incredible average speed of more than 130mph.

A few years ago I started to use a wide-angle lens more and more in my road racing photography so that I could go to places where the riders come close to the scenery and capture action close-up. This was not foolhardy – I sought out some protection and I did not want to put myself or anyone else in harm's way. But, as with anything when you push the limits, there is an element of risk. On this occasion I got too close. Or should I say Adrian Archibald got too close to me as he skimmed the wall on the TAS Suzuki at Guthries Memorial during practice for the 2004 TT. I had my head and lens above the wall when Adrian came in on a different line from anyone else, much closer to the wall. I had a split second to pull my head back as he passed through. It was a bit scary but if I have one picture that explains what it feels like to be at the TT this is it.

Curtains drawn against the sunshine, Jeremy Toye sits among the mundanities of motorhome life in the final moments before he heads to the start line for his first ever Isle of Man TT race. People tell the riders to 'go steady' and 'take it easy', but they are not going out there, they are not taking that terrifying drop down Bray Hill. Then, there is only the rider and the bike and their thoughts, dreams and fears of taking part in the greatest motorcycle racing challenge of them all. In a few moments the music will be gone, the only sound inside Toye's head will be the screaming engine and the rush of wind, and he will be confronted with every single one of those thoughts. Even from behind the camera it is chilling.

Sandwiched between the municipal cemetery and 'Gasoline Alley', Tim Reeves and Patrick Farrance cross the line on Glencrutchery Road to finish third in the 2008 Sidecar TT in their debut ride at the event.

WELCOME TO THE TT RACES

TT Sidecar Race 1   LEADERBOARD

MAXXIS TYRES

TT Sidecar Race 1

Steve Plater has the front wheel of the AIM Yamaha R1 pawing the air over Ago's Leap at 180mph during his first TT race, the Superbike event in 2007.

Proud father Steve Plater takes some time out from learning the TT course to nurse his baby daughter in the AIM Yamaha garage at the 2007 TT. Steve was a newcomer to the TT in 2007 but his six-week-old daughter Jazmin had already attended three race meetings before she travelled to the centenary TT with her dad.

Ramsey Bay is shining in the sunlight as Guy Martin climbs the Mountain road on the AIM Yamaha during the 2006 TT. As photographers and spectators we relish the opportunity to watch racing in such glorious surroundings but for the racers it rarely registers at all. I visited the Mountain section with Ian Lougher, Guy Martin and John McGuinness in the early winter of 2007 and they were all mesmerised by the view – they never have the chance to look back at a scene such as this as they concentrate on the stretch of road just in front of their wheel.

Avoiding all the obstacles that are part and parcel of a pure road race, John McGuinness (HM Plant Honda) has the evening sun on his back as he cranks through Guthrie's Memorial Bends during practice for the 2006 TT.

I like John McGuinness. Not just because he is a great road racer, one of the all-time great road racers. Nor because he always gives me a picture, making my job easy. No, it's more than that. John McGuinness lets you see what is going on inside his head, good and bad. He wears his heart on his sleeve and he isn't scared to show his vulnerability. The cameras are always there when you're winning – it's easy to smile when you're spraying the champagne, easy to give the quip to the scribblers. Not many people want to show their nerves before the race, to open a window on their self-doubt or dejection when they fail. But John has never shied away from showing these emotions publicly. He has let my camera in at times when a multitude of others might have said, 'Give my head a holiday'. This was one of those times. Nervous and edgy, struggling with the pressure of being expected to win the opening Superbike TT in 2006 as the 'works' Honda man, he still pulled on the leathers and let me see his build-up in his motorhome. It was all good stuff, the 'behind-the-scenes' opportunity, but then the main man delivered the main chance. He kissed the voodoo doll symbol on the back of his helmet, just a split-second thing he does before every race, to bring him luck and keep him safe. A special moment of privileged information that is treasured.

2008 was a difficult TT for the Flying Kiwi Bruce Anstey. He arrived on the island as an established star in the TAS Suzuki team with a new team-mate, Cameron Donald. Cameron was hungry for success, having missed the TT in 2007 through injury, and he immediately lived up to his promise by winning the opening two races of the week, the Superbike and Superstock TTs. The gauntlet was well and truly thrown down to

Bruce and by an Aussie to boot! The quietly spoken Kiwi hit back with
victory in the first Supersport TT but a technical infringement on his
bike saw him disqualified. Gutted, Bruce had to do it all again in the
second Supersport race and this time he made it stick, breaking every
record as he demolished the opposition. He is seen here on his way to
victory beneath the ancient stone walls at Tower Bends.

Literally flying over Ballacrye, Cameron Donald created a sensation in only his second TT in 2006 when he lapped at over 128mph and finished second in the Senior TT.

'Getting something different' is the first requirement of press photography, a golden rule that every picture editor preaches. After a fortnight of shooting the TT, that rule is tested to the utmost. By Senior day it can all get a bit jaded but you have to drive it on, keep the photographic throttle pinned wide open for that last lap. The 2006 Senior TT was a classic, held, like the whole fortnight's proceedings, in bright and glorious sunshine. I wanted a picture that could hint at that summeriness in some way and I thought it might make a nice picture if the top three finishers were enjoying an ice cream in the winner's enclosure. I arranged for the three cones to be brought over and I gave them to Bruce Anstey, Cameron Donald and John McGuinness. Cameron promptly pushed his cone into John's face and Bruce set his on top of John's head, making this happy shot. With that I grabbed the cones and the boys got up onto the rostrum for the traditional posed pictures for the rest of the snappers. Which brings us to the second rule of press photography – when you get something different make sure you're the only one who does!

2004 was the last time that 125cc two-stroke machines raced over the Mountain course in the final running of the Ultra-Lightweight TT. While Ian Lougher gave it everything he had on his Honda, some of the spectators outside the Raven pub in Ballaugh village seemed unimpressed that a moment of TT history was unfolding literally beneath their eyes.

Gary Johnson was a newcomer who wanted to make his mark in some way at the 2007 Centenary TT. Although he rode to some creditable finishes on the Ice Valley Yamaha, he will always be remembered as the guy who jumped Ballaugh Bridge one-handed during the Senior TT.

'Smile please!' A spectator captures the action as Ian Hutchinson hammers the AIM Yamaha into the Gooseneck during the second Supersport TT in 2008.

A classic TT scene as John McGuinness cranks the Padgett's Honda out of the Creg on his way to victory in the Senior in 2008. John had had a miserable fortnight until the final day when it all came good for him and he took his fourteenth TT win, equalling Mike Hailwood's tally and becoming the second most successful TT rider in history behind Joey Dunlop.

This was the last picture that I took at the 2008 Isle of Man TT and it is my favourite. John McGuinness, still in leathers a couple of hours after finishing the Senior TT and having spent some time meeting fans and signing autographs, raises the winner's trophy in front of the thousands of fans attending the prize-giving. It had been a wonderful TT with superb and safe racing. The Senior itself will go down in history as one of the great races with John and Cameron Donald locked in battle for the whole six laps.

Bush

Nestling in the narrow, bumpy lanes of County Tyrone, the Bush road races are the newest addition to the Irish road racing calendar. In 2008 the event was only in its third year, though the race has much earlier origins. The Dungannon and District Motorcycle Club, which organises the meeting, first ran the Dungannon 100 race back in 1924, and although that race is now history it provided the inspiration for the revived club to hold a new meeting on the 3.3-mile circuit around the tiny hamlet of Bush.

Tradition carries a great deal of weight in road racing. Before every meeting the national anthem is played and the spectators all around the course stand to attention in the hedges and remove their hats. For many other activities on the island, this would prove to be a politically contentious issue, but in road racing the tradition is happily acknowledged. At some events the race chaplain, a man charged with overseeing the spiritual welfare of the event (and in a sport that involves every aspect of life, including death, that is not as strange as it may sound), will say a public prayer for the safe running of the day's events a few minutes before the racing begins. As the bikes form up on the grid and the helpers move away, an official raises a '30 second' warning board, then, with 10 seconds to go, the 'Watch the Flag' board is shown, the national flag drops, and the race is under way.

The 125cc race sets off from the line at the 2008 Bush road races. The officials with the red flags are holding back two riders who will go in a second wave. Given the narrow roads only a certain number of machines are allowed to start the race together which often means there are three groups of riders starting a race at thirty-second intervals.

The narrow roads can be a bit of a problem when you have several 200bhp Superbikes battling for the same patch of tarmac at the start of a race. Paul Cranston (93, Cranston Fuels Honda) looks on as John Burrows (16, HM Motorhomes Suzuki) and Conor Cummins (49, JMF Millsport Yamaha) get tangled up at the start of the Open race at the 2007 Bush road races.

Raymond Porter (10, Donnan Yamaha) has only one wheel on the ground and Cameron Donald (86, Duncan Honda) has no contact with the road at all as they battle for the lead in the Open race at the 2006 Bush road races. The Bush race is notoriously bumpy. In 2008 Ryan Farquhar bent the footrest on his bike out of shape by the sheer pounding his bike suffered as it hammered over the uneven surface.

Athea

Motorcycle racing in general, and road racing on closed public roads in particular, are niche sports, getting little media attention outside of their own specialised press. A general observer might conclude that this lack of widespread media coverage comes from the fact that road racing is not a popular sport, but they would be wrong, as this picture from Athea road races in County Limerick highlights.

It is not only the big International meetings like the North West 200 and the Isle of Man TT that attract large crowds. The smaller meetings like Athea and Skerries are regularly attended by tens of thousands of people and yet, if you open a newspaper on the morning following a meeting, there often won't be any mention that the races even took place never mind a race report or results round-up!

Athea in west Limerick is the first race of the season to take place in the Republic of Ireland and with no other events in the vicinity it enjoys a unique position in a locality starved of motorcycle sport. Almost twenty thousand people descend upon the tiny village every year to watch the racers do battle around a 3.3-mile course that passes a holy well and is so narrow in one stretch that two cars cannot pass each other without taking to the grass.

After a disastrous start in 2002, when the inaugural Athea meeting was washed out by torrential rain before it had even begun, the road races have become an important factor in the rejuvenation of a deprived local community. The Athea meeting brings an estimated € 1 million into the local economy and its success has led to a range of other community activities there, including vintage vehicle rallies and traditional music festivals.

While road racing may be something of an anachronism in the twenty-first century in its attitudes to health and safety, facilities or media involvement, it is very much in tune with its historical geography. These small out-of-the-way places in Ireland and elsewhere can enjoy the benefits of a sport that is run on a voluntary basis by resourceful people who employ a 'can do' attitude to organise the events for the sheer enjoyment and satisfaction of doing so.

A huge crowd make their way home after a fine day's racing at Athea in June 2005.

Racers like Shane Connor (Suzuki) pass under the very noses of the crowds of fans gathered on the banks at Paddock Bend during the 2005 Athea road races.

Darran Lindsay (Noel Johnston Honda) signals for the race to be stopped during a torrential downpour as he rounds Village Corner in the 600cc event at the 2006 Athea races. The meeting was subsequently abandoned. All road racing suffers from the vagaries of the weather and in recent years safety considerations have seen organisers no longer willing to run wet races.

Making her way past the trees in Athea village during the Junior Classic race at the 2005 meeting, Elle Forrest is one of only a handful of female riders in road racing. Raised in Scotland, Elle is now based in Ireland where she can pursue her racing. She is part of a racing migration that has developed over the years now that Ireland and the Isle of Man are the only parts of these islands where public road closing orders are allowed.

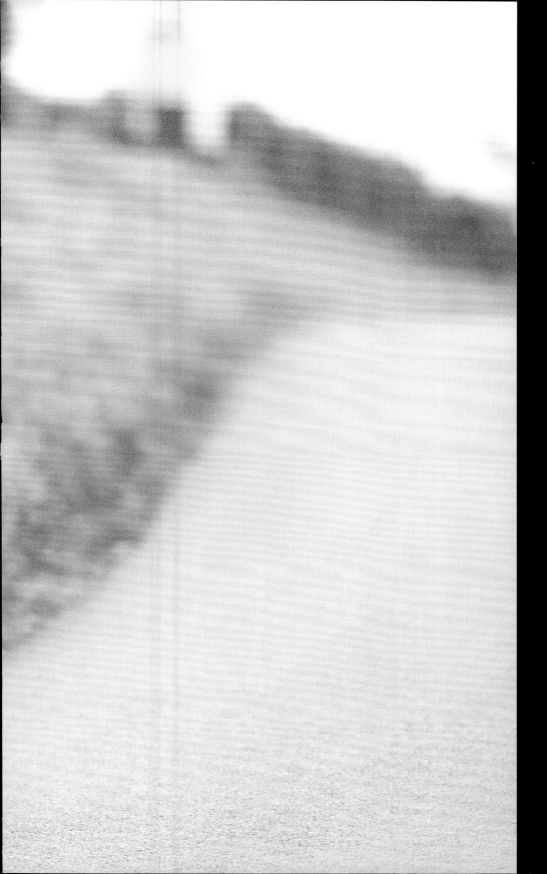

Skerries
100

The most famous of all the races in the South, Skerries takes its name from the County Dublin seaside village where the first race began on Main Street in July 1946. The same area had played host to the Leinster 200 in the 1930s, a race in which legendary names like Walter Rusk, Stanley Woods and Jimmy Guthrie competed. Steeped in history, today's race draws over thirty thousand spectators to the 2.92-mile course that lies between the villages of Lusk and Skerries.

The race is often called 'Scary Skerries' as the combination of high-speed lap times on the narrow, bumpy circuit and the continuous lines of spectators sitting only a few feet away from the frantic action creates an unsettling feeling that everything is too dangerously close together.

The great thrill of road racing is our proximity to the speed of the race and there are few places to get as close to that speed as Skerries. At places like Sam's Tunnel or Duke's Bends we are only a few feet away from racers' fairings clashing at way over 100mph. Every sense is electrified into life by the spectacle. There is an appalling fascination in watching, hearing, smelling, even tasting the danger of the battle: while everyone knows what can go wrong we are simultaneously amazed at the skill of the racers in controlling the mayhem.

Barry Maguire kicks up the dust on the Lilley Suzuki as he runs out of tarmac at the bottom of Gillies Leap during the 2005 Skerries 100.

He came, he saw, he conquered. Cameron Donald made his first visit to Skerries in 2006 and he left with a double victory in the Open race and the Grand Final as well as race and lap records, including the outright lap record for the course. The Australian's exploits won the hearts of the crowd who gave him a standing ovation at Dublin Road Corner.

There is no other race where the crowds get as close to the action as they do at Skerries. Sam Dunlop (Honda) chases David Brown (Honda) out of Dublin Road Corner during the 125cc race at the 2005 meeting.

Southern
100

The Billown course on the outskirts of the Isle of Man port of Castletown hosts several race meetings a year, including the Pre-TT Classic and Post-TT Steam Packet events, but it is the Southern 100 meeting, held there in the second week of July over the 4.25-mile circuit, that is the most prestigious.

Known in the sport as the 'friendly races', the Southern is run in a much more easy-going way than the TT and the inclusion of two practice days as well as evening racing allows the racers time to relax into the event. The meeting was run in this spirit from the outset in 1955 when the competitors and officials of the three-race programme took part in a gymkhana in Castletown stadium after the racing was over!

One of the last places that still runs sidecar racing on a National course, Billown has a fearsome reputation as almost all of its length is bordered by solid stone walls. Some of those walls come in the shape of the picturesque cottages at the wonderfully named Ballabeg, Ballawhetstone and Cross Four Ways.

Manxman Conor Cummins tucks his JMF Millsport Yamaha underneath the walls at Church Bends during the Open championship race at the Southern 100 in 2007.

Ian Lougher (Black Horse Yamaha) holds off Ryan Farquhar (Harker Kawasaki) at Castletown Corner on his way to victory in the 600cc race during the 2008 Southern 100 meeting. Lougher became the most successful ever Southern 100 rider in 2008 with three wins taking him to a tally of thirty-two, one more than the previous record holder, Joey Dunlop.

Chris Palmer (Mannin Honda) leads Ian Lougher (Jackson Honda) past the cottage at Cross Four Ways Corner during the wet 125cc race at the 2008 meeting. Lougher won the race from Palmer.

Walderstown

From the 1970s through to the mid-1990s the 'Race of the South', as it was known, was run on the old Fore village course in County Westmeath in the Irish Republic. Fore was first run in 1973 and the winner of the 350cc race that day was Michael Laverty, father of Eugene, John and Michael Laverty who are all top track racers of the current era. In 2000 the meeting was switched to the Walderstown course, just a stone's throw from Athlone.

At just two miles long Walderstown is the shortest course in Irish road racing. Almost all of the newer races in Ireland are run on shorter courses as it causes fewer issues with residents and businesses and requires fewer personnel to man the course on practice and race days.

Running a race on closed public roads throws up problems that few of us would ever consider. I watched with some amusement at Walderstown recently as a bread delivery man negotiated with Gardai and marshals to be allowed to bring his van on to the course between race sessions to make his delivery to the local shop!

In some places in Ireland you don't even have to leave your front door to watch the racing. Ryan Farquhar (Harker Kawasaki) chases Barry Maguire (Lilley Suzuki) and Damien Mulleady (DM Racing Yamaha) around the old RIC station at Walderstown Crossroads during the 2005 meeting.

William Dunlop (Flynn Honda) has no time to pop into the shop as he outbrakes his brother Michael (Honda) and Barry Davidson (CB Racing Honda) into Corr Crossroads during the 250cc race at the 2008 Walderstown meeting.

Richard Britton (P.J. O'Kane Suzuki) and Ryan Farquhar (Harker Kawasaki) give each other the thumbs-up in a sign of mutual respect after a hard-fought superbike battle in the Open race at Walderstown in 2004.

Kells

Kells road race course is about one thing – jumps. The 2.2-mile course in the village of Crossakiel, County Meath, is home to the two most spectacular leaps in Irish road racing – O'Dea's Milestone on the run up to the last corner and Hanlon's Leap on the drop down from the start and finish line.

In 2007 the telemetry on Cameron Donald's Honda Fireblade indicated that he was hitting 157mph as he took off from the jump at O'Dea's. The bikes are thrown five or six feet up into the air and travel for 20 to 30 yards before they land, compressing the suspension to its limit and grinding away the bottom of the fairings. The spectators are sitting in the hedge only a few feet away from this incredible action and these attractions have helped to build Kells into the most successful National Irish road race in the calendar.

A classic Irish road racing scene as Dave Coughlan and Barry Maguire lead a group of riders down the drop to Hanlon's Leap in front of hedges packed with spectators

Faugheen
50

The return of racing to the Faugheen circuit in County Tipperary represents part of the revival in motorcycle road racing in the Republic of Ireland over the past decade. This resurgence coincided with the rise of Martin Finnegan as a star from the South who could take on and beat the top racers from the North like Adrian Archibald, Ryan Farquhar, Richard Britton and Darran Lindsay. Not since Eddie Laycock in the late 1980s had the Republic had a rider who could achieve that, and while Laycock was a brilliant racer he did not have the spectacular style and charisma of the young man from Lusk.

Racing did take place in Faugheen, a tiny hamlet that consists of little more than a handful of houses grouped around a church, a pub and a shop, from 1976 until 1986, when it ended due to a lack of resources. A club was formed in the area in 2001 and racing returned again to the 2.3-mile circuit in 2003.

The country lanes were so bumpy that racing was confined to machines no bigger than 600cc for the first few years of the competition until some resurfacing work was carried out. Nowadays the Faugheen 50 hosts rounds of all the Irish championship classes.

The road seems to nestle in the County Tipperary landscape as Cathal Whelan (Kawasaki) leads Keith Costello (Yamaha) and Declan O'Meara (Yamaha) into Faugheen village during the 2006 meeting.

A phenomenal racing season is coming to an end in these pictures. Cameron Donald, who had won races and set lap records at almost every race he had turned up at in 2006, has just been high-sided off the Duncan Honda at Chapel Corner in Faugheen. The force is pushing him across the road where, compressed between bike and kerb, Cameron snapped vertebrae in his back, bringing his racing to a premature end for the year.

It looked like the most innocuous of crashes. The speed was out of the impact by this stage and watching through the camera, I expected him to jump up on to his feet and run away. But it wasn't to be.

The shower of rain that had preceded the race had been quickly followed by intense sunshine that had dried the road in minutes. Or most of it. Around the village corner there was only a narrow, bone-dry line, maybe three feet wide, that race leader Ray Porter had steered through on lap one. Outside that line there were scattered damp patches, ready to trap the unwary. Cameron, seeking more drive out of the corner, was running wider and leaning further over on this part of the road as he gave chase. It looked dodgy and I changed to a looser optic for the second lap. These are the pictures of what I feared might happen. Fortunately Cameron has now made a complete recovery.

Mid Antrim
150

Sadly the Mid Antrim 150 is one of the races that has disappeared from the road racing calendar in recent times. Internal administrative problems led to the abandonment of the 2008 meeting just a year after the event had celebrated its sixtieth anniversary. The Mid Antrim was one of the few races to run during the 2001 outbreak of foot-and-mouth disease that led to the cancellation of almost all rural activities that summer.

Since 1946 the race had seen various course changes before ending up on the Clough circuit that passed through the little County Antrim village. The old Rathkenny circuit, used until the 1990s, had presented a true road racer's challenge, but the final 3.5-mile course had a charm all of its own as it took the riders around the village church and down over the spectacular Alexander's Leap.

No one knows if the Mid Antrim will ever run again but it would be sad if the course where Joey Dunlop won his cherished first trophy, a tiny cup for finishing in fifth place on a 200c Suzuki in the 1972 meeting, has gone for good from the racing season.

Local man Jeff Shaw steers his 125cc Honda around Clough church in the heart of the County Antrim village during the 2005 meeting. The painted kerbs, flags and bunting are part of Northern Ireland's Twelfth of July celebrations.

William Dunlop (Honda) shaves the grass on the bank at O'Hara's Bend during the 250cc race at the 2005 Mid Antrim 150. I watched the riders at this corner in the practice session the evening before and I was certain that during the race, when they were pushing a little harder, someone would brush against the bank. I returned in the morning and crawled into a hole in the ditch to wait.

William's father Robert Dunlop (KES Aprilia) leads his great rival Marc Curtin (Honda) out of Clough Hairpin on his way to victory in the 125cc race at the 2007 Mid Antrim 150. The village residents and shopkeepers can watch from their doorsteps as the action unfolds.

Ulster Grand Prix

In 2007 John McGuinness lapped Dundrod at 131.717mph to make the Ulster Grand Prix course not just the fastest road race but also the fastest motorcycle race in the world. And John didn't even win the race!

Dundrod has always been loved for its fast-flowing sweeps and hated for its all too often awful weather. The 7.4-mile course is perched on the top of the hills on the outskirts of Belfast in County Antrim, attracting the rain clouds as well as the world's top road racers. From its inception in 1922 until 1971 the Ulster Grand Prix was a world championship Grand Prix and its list of previous winners is a who's who of motorcycle racing down through the ages: Woods, Duke, Surtees, Hailwood, Agostini, Taveri, Ivy, Redman, Read, Herron and Dunlop.

The shift away from public roads circuits for the Grand Prix circus sidelined races like the Ulster and the TT and forced a shift of direction for these events. They have survived by emphasising their history as unique races on closed public roads and there will always be riders who want to experience that challenge and spectators who want to come and watch them do so.

Spectators lean over a rusty gate at Budore to catch a fleeting glimpse of Bruce Anstey (TAS Suzuki) lead John McGuinness (Hawk Kawasaki) through the 170mph right-hander during the Superbike race at the 2004 Ulster Grand Prix. Anstey was in indomitable form that year, winning three races and setting an absolute course record.

With Slemish mountain in the distance, a gaggle of screaming strokers start the stomach-churning descent of the Deer's Leap during the 250cc race at the 2005 Ulster Grand Prix.

As you come over the top of the Leap, the road falls away from beneath you so abruptly that you cannot see any sign of tarmac, just acres and acres of empty sky. It is one of those places that must be committed to and taken on blind faith. At 150mph. And then, as soon as the bike is around the corner, it stands up on its end and shakes its head as Ian Hutchinson's HM Plant Honda is doing here during the 2007 Ulster Grand Prix.

The fastest corner on the fastest course in the world has no name. It doesn't even look like much of a corner at normal road speeds, just a slight right kink between Jordan's Cross and the Hole in the Wall. Flat-out in top gear, it turns into an awesomely fast bend that is made all the more difficult when the bumps throw the front wheel into the air at over 180mph as Ian Lougher's Stobart Honda is doing here during the 2006 Ulster Grand Prix. When you photograph here, and I heartily recommend that you do not, it is really scary to watch the bikes drifting across the road towards you as they lose traction and the back wheel spins up on the edge of the tyre.

David Jefferies (V&M Yamaha) rushes between the hedges at Ireland's Bend to a brace of victories in the Superbike races at the 2000 Ulster Grand Prix. David's first year competing at the Prix was 1999, which most people remember as the year that Joey Dunlop beat David to win his last ever Dundrod race, but David himself had made an amazing debut. Riding with a damaged wrist, he won the opening Superbike race, had a spectacular crash in the 600cc race at Wheeler's Bend and left Dundrod as the absolute lap record holder with a lap of 126.85mph, beating Joey's lap time by one-tenth of a second.

Uel Duncan's elbow is only an inch from the bank as he cranks the Robinson Honda through Tournagrough during the Dundrod 150 meeting in 2000. Forced to retire from racing through injury following a crash at the Ulster Grand Prix later in the season, Uel now runs his own highly successful road race team.

Quarry Bends has been remodelled since I took this picture of Adrian Archibald on the TAS Suzuki during the Dundrod 150 in 2003. (The Dundrod 150 replaced the old Killinchy 150 meeting held on the same course and the event is now incorporated into the Ulster Grand Prix Bike Week.) The hedge has been removed and the corner smoothed out a little with kerbs and new fencing. It is probably safer now but is one less place where I can stick my lens through a hole in the hedge and capture the action as the bikes slide past. The pursuit of safety is paramount in the world's most dangerous sport and the changes that brings mean that images like this become even more special because they can never be taken again.

On Saturday 19 August 2006 Darran Lindsay stood on the top step of the podium at the Ulster Grand Prix, flanked by William Dunlop and Ian Lougher whom he had just beaten to win the 250cc race. It was a very, very happy day for Darran. He lived only a few hundred yards from the podium, making this an emphatic win on his home course and his family were there to celebrate his success.

That happiness was shattered just three weeks later on 9 September when Darran was killed in a crash during practice at the Killalane road races in County Dublin. Four days later Darran's funeral cortege left his home and made its way down to the start and finish area of the Ulster Grand Prix. The pallbearers stopped at the pole position marker that Darran had occupied just a few weeks before. Other than the sound of the rain falling on the hard road, there was total silence.

Road racing is defined by those two days, caught between the joy of victory and the happiness it brings to men who live to race and the unspeakable sadness that is left when they perish living that life.

John McGuinness splashes the HM Plant Honda past soaked spectators at Tournagrough, just moments before the 2007 Ulster Grand Prix was abandoned following a deluge. Dundrod is famous for its awful weather and in 2007 it lived up to that reputation. Heavy rain and driving wind lashed spectators and racers alike from early morning and it seemed as if the meeting would be over before it had begun: standing water on the road dictated that the race could not be run in the interests of safety. However, the rain eased and after a delay most of the races were run before the heavens opened again in the afternoon and the action was brought to a premature end. Although little can be done about the weather, it can have disastrous consequences for the meeting. In 2008, the Ulster Grand Prix was cancelled for the first time in its history because of the torrential rain. Road races require a great deal of money to be laid out in advance of the event and few organising clubs have any cash reserve. The hope is that the money can be recouped on the day through programme sales, admission charges and so on. It is a hand-to-mouth existence and if racing has to be cancelled because of bad weather the organising club, and hence the race, can be bankrupted.

Spectators huddle beneath their brollies for protection from the driving rain at Quarry Bends in 2007.

I took this photograph of Joey Dunlop on his RC45 Honda during practice for the 1999 Ulster Grand Prix from exactly the spot where I watched my first ever road race twenty-five years previously. Joey had been racing that day too as I watched at the end of the Cochranstown Straight on the approach to Quarterlands. It was the start of what was to be a brilliant career for Joey and a long love affair with road racing for me.

1999 was to be Joey's last year at Dundrod and he won the final race he ever rode on the course, claiming victory in the Superbike race. His brother Robert also won the last race that he competed in at Dundrod, the 125cc race in 2007. Robert is seen here leading Ian Lougher through Joey's Windmill Corner on his way to victory.

Manx Grand Prix

When what is now known as the Manx Grand Prix was first run in 1923 it was called the 'Amateur TT'. 'Amateur' meant that the thirty-three riders and their machines had no manufacturer's support or reward and that ethos has been maintained for the Manx (which changed its name in 1930) ever since. Only competitors who are resident in the British Isles and who have not competed in other international races are allowed to enter the August event, though these rules are now to be relaxed as speeds increase at the TT and slower riders are being encouraged to race in the Manx instead.

Run over the same Mountain course as the TT, the Manx is a much quieter event that attracts only a small crowd, many of whom are directly involved with the racing. It is very much a hands-on event and the paddock is populated with small vans and caravans rather than race transporters and mobile homes.

A big part of the Manx racing nowadays involves 'classic' bikes, machines from another era that are still raced by a dedicated bunch of enthusiasts, making the Manx the most important race of this type in the world. This gives the race much of its old-world charm that harks back to a simpler time in motorcycle racing and fits wonderfully with the nostalgic surroundings of the Isle of Man and its unique two-wheeled racing heritage.

Race winner Craig Atkinson douses runner-up Derek Brien with champagne on the podium after the Senior Manx Grand Prix in 2006. Craig had just scored a double, having already beaten Derek in the Junior race two days before. The duo dominated 2006 race week.

An old classic machine that has succumbed to the rigours of competition on the Mountain course in the Senior Classic Manx Grand Prix is left parked against a lamppost at The Nook in 2007.

Craig Atkinson (2, Honda) and Derek Brien (1, Kawasaki) cross the line together in the closest ever finish in over one hundred years of racing on the Isle of Man. The two riders had set off together (at the Manx the riders leave the line in pairs unlike the TT's individual starts) and after 150 miles of racing and a pit stop they were only separated by one hundreth of a second. Atkinson was declared the winner of the photo finish and even the chequered-flag man celebrated the momentous occasion!

Dundalk

Dundalk road races in County Louth have been an on–off affair in recent years and in many ways they epitomise the problems that road race organisers face. Resistance, including legal action, from residents and local authorities has forced the organisers to relocate the race to other courses or to be cancelled altogether in some years. Races have been run through Dundalk town itself, along the main Belfast–Dublin artery on the edge of town, and on surrounding country lanes, but no matter where they have travelled to, the organisers have run into problems.

Careful diplomacy is the name of the game for most Clerks of the Course in Ireland as they try to balance the needs of local businesses and residents with the running of a race over two days. The proprietors of a multitude of rural enterprises have to be cajoled into shutting down operations for the day. Residents living on the course must be persuaded that they are willing participants in a local festival of speed rather than prisoners in their own homes for the weekend.

But perhaps the greatest threat to the sport is litigation. Legal responsibility for any failing in the modern world can end up in a court of law with a claim for compensation. In road racing, which is run on an amateur basis, this poses the greatest danger. Road racing can only be made safer, never safe. Road racers are as unwilling as ever to be beaten and, as bikes get faster and speeds increase, these minor roads become arenas for high-speed battles where one small error or mechanical failure can lead to disaster.

While the dangers to the racers are omnipresent, understood, and accepted by all involved, road racing, in brutally honest terms, cannot organise and promote events, encourage people to come along to watch, and then allow those spectators to be harmed. At the 2007 Isle of Man TT two spectators were killed and two marshals badly injured in a horrific accident. Aside from the terrible cost to these individuals and their families, the repercussions for the event have been severe in terms of legal action and insurance costs and have brought the sport to a crossroads. It is now clear that if road racing cannot prove that it can prevent such tragedies from occurring in the future, then it may not have a future at all.

Spectators watch only inches from the roadside as Ryan Farquhar leaps the Harker Kawasaki over the infamous Darver Jump in 2005.

It is said that every self-respecting Irish road race course must incorporate at least one pub in its length and the Readypenny Inn forms a colourful backdrop to the start of the 250cc race at the Dundalk road races in 2004.

Guy Martin leaps the Duncan Suzuki over Darver Jump during the Open race at Dundalk in 2004. In the biggest jump in Irish road racing at that time, the bikes were thrown six feet up into the air as the road dropped away beneath them.

Scarborough

The first time I photographed at Oliver's Mount, home of the Scarborough event, Guy Martin came around the Esses, leaning over so far that he had his elbow in the grass and I could see the plastic being ground away in a cloud of dust from his knee slider. I only stayed at that spot for one lap!

Scarborough is England's only natural roads circuit. Set in wooded parkland, the course is perched precariously on the steep slopes above the Yorkshire seaside town and plays host to several meetings a year, including the Spring Cup, the Cock O' the North and the Gold Cup events.

The races have their origins in the town corporation's desire to host a 'Welcome Home' week for returning servicemen after World War Two. The stone tracks of the park were tarred over in a few weeks and the first races held on the 2.5-mile course in September 1946. Racing has continued every year since.

Welshman Ian Lougher is the most successful Scarborough racer of all time with over one hundred wins at the Yorkshire circuit. Ian is one of a long list of illustrious Scarborough winners that includes Geoff Duke, John Surtees, Phil Read, Giacomo Agostini, Barry Sheene, Carl Fogarty and David Jefferies.

Between 1994 and 2004 Phillip McCallen held the outright lap record for Scarborough, until he was bettered by the modern master of the Mount, Guy Martin, the only rider in history to win the Gold Cup five years in succession.

John McGuinness (1, Hawk Kawasaki) and Ryan Farquhar (77, Harker Kawasaki) act as road sweepers as they clear the autumn leaves from the Mere Hairpin during the 2004 Gold Cup meeting at Scarborough.

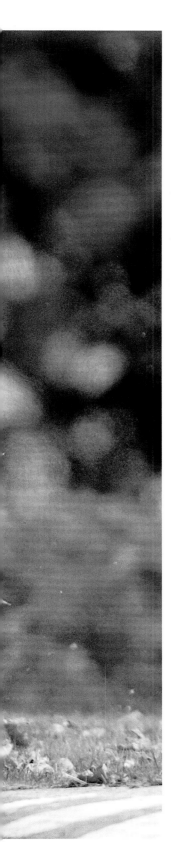

The bikes take their places on the grid for the start of the 125cc race at the 2004 Gold Cup event last Scarborough. From the start the racers blast down to the Mere Hairpin before beginning a steep climb to the Esses and the top section of Oliver's Mount. Two short straights and two hairpin bends take the bikes back down the mountain to the lower section. This narrow, twisty track still plays host to sidecar racing.

The grass flies as Ian Hutchinson (Kawasaki) gets his knee down at the Esses in 2004. The Bingley rider has taken a place in the highest echelon of road racing with wins at all of the International meetings in recent years, including a Supersport TT victory in 2007.

Killalane

The Killalane road races are the sister event of the Skerries 100, and both events are organised by the Loughshinny Motorcycle Club. Traditionally the Irish season's curtain-closer, the Killalane meeting shares the same paddock and part of the 3.6-mile County Dublin course with the July meeting. What it does not share with Skerries is a tree planted in the middle of the road on one corner, the infamous Kearney's Tree. Apparently, there used to be a more mature tree at this spot when the course was run in an anti-clockwise direction and the riders were headed straight for it when they were braking!

Being run on closed public highways, road races have to incorporate all kinds of local landmarks into their courses. Whitewashed cottages, old Gardai stations, petrol stations, shops, pubs, hotels, tearooms, farmyards, schools, churches and holy wells are just some of the 'obstacles' that are to be found around road race circuits in these islands. While these places are often picturesque and provide wonderful backdrops for photographs, they also create obvious dangers for the riders.

Competitors in the Classic race make their way past Kearney's Tree during the 2003 Killalane races.

Anyone who met Richard Britton will tell you that he was always laughing or smiling. He was a man at ease with the world, naturally happy, who always saw his glass as half-full rather than half-empty. Often the victim of bad luck or unreliable machinery, the Enniskillen man never became despondent. It was obvious that he loved racing and he rose above any misfortune, making light of it in his jovial way as he moved on to the next race.

Richard was not only one of Ireland's top road racers but also probably the most popular. Fellow racers and fans alike warmed to his brilliance on the bike and to his humility and good humour off it. It was a huge shock for everyone when he lost his life in a freak crash at Ballybunion, in County Kerry, in September 2005. Richard's carefree spirit had made him seem immune to that kind of tragedy. Only a week before his death he had been smiling over at my camera at Killalane as he wheelied past in celebration after winning what was to be his last race.

The spectators are only a couple of feet away from Conor Cummins as he hammers past them at over 140mph during the Killalane road races in 2007.

The sign says 'Mind Our Children, Drive Carefully' as Guy Martin steers the Duncan Suzuki between the telegraph poles on the back section of the Killalane course in 2004.

Boyne

In 2006 the Tullyallen Motorcycle Club revived the Boyne road races in the area made famous by the battle fought along the banks of the County Meath river in 1690. The race course was a mixture of incredibly fast 'A' roads and a tiny twisting section called King William's Glen, in memory of the events that took place there.

While for many people from outside Ireland the political and religious divisions on the island have been mystifying, they have been very real and destructive for those who have had to live with them. Sport has not escaped these splits and the divisions have ripped many activities apart. That has not been the case in motorcycle racing, where such pressures have rarely had any impact. Throughout most of the years of the Northern Ireland Troubles road racing continued to take place and racers and fans alike travelled from all parts of the island to all other parts of the island, regardless of borders, to compete in and watch the racing.

The non-sectarian nature of road racing was perhaps best summed up at Richard Britton's funeral in 2005. The funeral cortege left the Enniskillen racer's home to walk through the streets of the County Fermanagh town to the chapel where a Roman Catholic funeral Mass was held and taken part in by everyone present. Afterwards the sad procession moved on to the cemetery and when Richard was buried the priest invited all of the mourners to come to a local Protestant church hall for refreshments. In a land divided for so long, that sad day effortlessly crossed the ancient divisions in memory of a man who gave so much pleasure to everyone from every background.

Caught in a shaft of light filtering down through the trees in King William's Glen, Wayne Kirwan (Donnan Yamaha) is on his way to victory in the Support race at the 2006 Boyne road races.

Sam Dunlop leads Des Butler up through King William's Glen during the 250cc race in the 2006 Boyne road races. The Glen road is fascinating as this mile of the course is devoid of almost any kind of protection for the riders. The stones beside Sam Dunlop are painted white simply to warn the racers that they are there.

Race organisers rely upon the goodwill of the local residents and farmers – they need access and assistance, they need permissions and paddocks. But the goodwill of God is often harder to rely upon when it comes to the fickle Irish weather. A week of heavy rain turned the barley stubble of Boyne into a quagmire, a pool of glar that the racers like Michael Dunlop had to wheel their bikes through on the way to and from the start line.

Macau Grand Prix

When you wake up in the morning in a Macau hotel the first thing you hear is the wail of race bikes as they scythe between the skyscrapers on the streets of the densely packed city. The Macau Grand Prix, run on a 3.8-mile course in the former Portuguese colony in China, has the unique distinction of being the only motorcycle race run through a city. Regarded as a season-end holiday race by most of the road racing fraternity, the bikes have been racing the Guia course each November since 1966.

If you are still in bed when you hear that sound you have missed at least a quarter of the bike racing that you travelled to China to watch, as the bikes, regarded as the poor cousins of the car racing brigade that dominates the week-long race festival, only get a couple of early morning practice sessions before the race.

Macau is an incredible spectacle as a motorcycle race, the most exciting place I have ever watched racing, but only if you have a photographer's pass that allows you to get down to the side of the road behind the miles of Armco barriers that line the circuit. If you look closely at the photographs here you will see they are almost completely devoid of spectators. Stern-looking policeman and an army of marshals ensure that no one stops by the trackside to watch, moving everyone along to the only places they are allowed to spectate from – remote and soulless grandstands at the start and finish area and at Lisboa Bend.

The level of that enforcement is both frustrating and understandable. It is probably the only way that the officials could safely cope with running a race through the streets of one of the most densely populated cities in the world. But a major part of road racing for spectators is that they can get close to the action on closed public roads, feel the speed and share the adrenaline rush of the racers. In Macau the people are kept remote from the action and today very few local people seem interested in the racing. It is much more an event for tourists that inconveniences their daily lives.

In Ireland and the Isle of Man, road racing's spiritual homes, road race fans have always been enthusiastically involved in the sport as part of the culture of their local areas. Many volunteer to help out with the running of the meetings. Farmers around the courses allow access to their land for spectating and car parking. Thousands more attend on practice and race days to feel the thrill that comes from the close proximity to the incredible speed and skill of the racers. In an age when experience is increasingly of the virtual variety, road racing is the real deal, raw and dangerously exciting.

It is that danger and its implications that continue to thrust road racing into a debate about its future. The difference between the Macau photographs and the earlier Skerries images in this book is immense, not from the point of view of the rider who is putting his life on the line in both places, but from the spectator's vantage point. In a sense that difference is symbolic of the crossroads at which road racing as a sport now stands. Will the increasing risk of harm to spectators, in an era of intense concern for health and safety, and the threat of litigation if things do go wrong, mean a shift from the close-up thrills of County Dublin to the empty spaces of Macau for all of us?

And if that does happen, will it be worth going road racing at all?

Casting a lonely shadow the road, a lone racer passes a cemetery on the hill section of the Guia course in Macau in 2006.

There is no margin for error as Michael Rutter guides the Stobart Honda down through the Armco tunnel during the 2006 Macau Grand Prix. Six-time Macau winner, Michael shares the record for most wins with Ron Haslam.

Steve Plater has the AIM Yamaha on its side as he negotiates Melcoo Hairpin, the tightest corner in motorcycle racing anywhere in the world, during practice for the 2006 Macau Grand Prix.

Dwarfed by the huge skyscrapers, Stephan Mertens (Suzuki) is followed around Melcoo Hairpin by Ian Lougher (Slingshot Honda) and Cameron Donald (Honda) during the 2005 Macau Grand Prix. A 600cc race for machines like the one Cameron is riding is incorporated into the main race and a separate trophy is awarded to the winner.

A local man is on his way to work as Portuguese racer Nuno Silva exits Moorish Hill on his Kawasaki during practice for the 2005 Macau Grand Prix. The footpath remains open to allow people to move around but if the man had stopped to watch the bikes through the fence he would have been quickly moved along by the Macanese police. They do not allow anyone to spectate from the side of the track.

A race marshal lights incense sticks and places them into cracks in the concrete walls at Guia Bend to ward off danger on the Macau course before the start of the first practice session at the 2006 event. Other than this appeal to the gods and a few mattresses thrown against the barriers at some corners when the bikes are in action, Macau offers no protection to the racers. They remain sanguine about the risks; when Macau regular Stephen Thompson saw this picture he quipped with characteristic black humour, 'Oh good, now we can get our eyes poked out by sticks too when we fall off!'

American racer John Haner ducks under the Armco as he exits the final bend on his Honda during the 2006 Macau Grand Prix.

You can get closer to the action with a camera at Macau than anywhere else in the world as the riders pass within a few inches of the barriers. When I knelt down to peer between the rails at John McGuinness on his Stobart Honda in 2005 the dust and dirt he kicked up blew through the gap into my eyes.

I closed my eyes as I took this picture, watching the two-inch needle being pushed into Mark Miller's cracked rib to deposit the painkiller that would allow him to race in the Macau Grand Prix in 2006. The doctor went from garage to garage doing this, injecting arms and backsides, legs and torsos.

There is very little daylight between Callum Ramsey's right shoulder and the barrier as he plunges down the hill into the Macau streets at over 90mph on the MSS Discovery Kawasaki.

And there is probably even less daylight between John McGuinness's helmet and the edge of this concrete wall as he exits the Solitude Esses on the Stobart Honda during the 2006 Macau Grand Prix. In recent years the Macau race has become extremely competitive and in the relentless search for speed the racers are riding ever closer to the walls and barriers.

Ian Hutchinson is rubbing his helmet against the metal barrier as he dives down into Macau city on the Stobart Honda during the 2006 Macau Grand Prix. There are bolts in Armco barriers that hold the guard rails to the uprights and the racers are terrified of them. I have heard them talk fearfully about how dangerous it is to catch your leathers on the bolt heads but in the same breath they say it isn't so bad to brush your shoulders against the yellow walls because the cement is smooth.

Steve Plater celebrates winning the 2006 Macau Grand Prix with a burnout on his AIM Yamaha as he returns to the paddock.

Stephen Davison has been a road racing fan since he attended his first race in 1974 and is a regular contributor to *MCN*. He is the author of the bestselling books *Joey Dunlop: King of the Roads*, *Beautiful Danger*, *Ragged Edge*, *Hard Roads*, *Flying Finn*, *Between the Hedges*, *John McGuinness TT Legend* and *Road Racers*. Davison has been the recipient of a number of photographic awards, including Northern Ireland Sports Photographer of the Year and Northern Ireland Press Photographer of the Year. He is the joint owner of the prestigious photographic agency Pacemaker Press.

Front cover: Cameron Donald leaps O'Dea's Jump on the Duncan Honda at Kells in 2007
Back cover: Lined up on the grid at Walderstown in 2006

First published in 2008 by Blackstaff Press

This edition published, with corrections, in 2015 by
Blackstaff Press
4D Weavers Court
Linfield Road
Belfast
BT12 5GH

Printed in Northern Ireland by W&G Baird

A CIP record for this book is available from the British Library

ISBN 978-085640-964-6

www.blackstaffpress.com
www.pacemakerpressintl.com